FIRST BIOGRAPHIES

Booker T. Washington

Trade Edition published 1995 © Steck-Vaughn Company.
Copyright © 1995 Steck-Vaughn Company.

Published by Raintree Steck-Vaughn Publishers, an imprint of Steck-Vaughn Company

Retold for young readers by Edith Vann
Editor: Pam Wells
Project Manager: Julie Klaus
Electronic Production: Scott Melcer

Library of Congress Cataloging-in-Publication Data

Gleiter, Jan, 1947-
    Booker T. Washington / Jan Gleiter and Kathleen Thompson.
      p.   cm. — (First biographies)
    ISBN 0-8114-8454-8 hardcover library binding
    ISBN 0-8114-9353-9 softcover binding
    1. Washington, Booker T., 1856-1915 — Juvenile literature.
2. Afro-Americans — Biography — Juvenile literature.   3. Educators —
United States — Biography — Juvenile literature.   [1. Washington,
Booker T., 1856-1915. 2. Educators. 3. Afro-Americans —
Biography.]   I. Thompson, Kathleen. II. Title. III. Series.
E185.97.W4G543   1995
370'.92 — dc20   94-41001
[B]   CIP   AC

Printed and bound in the United States
  0 W 04 03 02 01

FIRST
BIOGRAPHIES

Booker T. Washington

Jan Gleiter and Kathleen Thompson
Illustrated by Rick Whipple

RSVP

RAINTREE
STECK-VAUGHN
PUBLISHERS
The Steck-Vaughn Company

Austin, Texas

It was spring 1856 in Virginia. A boy was born on a large farm called a plantation. His family belonged to the family that owned the plantation. So this little boy was a slave. His name was Booker.

Booker, his mother, and his brother, John, lived in a small cabin. It had a dirt floor and windows with no glass. There were holes in the walls. Later Booker's sister, Amanda, was born.

Often there wasn't any food in the mornings. Booker ate boiled corn put out for the farm animals. He had only one thing to wear—a long itchy, burlap shirt. When he grew too large for it, he got another. But he never had more than one shirt at a time.

Booker hated the shirts when they were new and rough. They made him scratch. They hurt his skin. Luckily for Booker, his big brother was kind. He would wear Booker's new shirts for him. This way he wore off the part that hurt with his own skin.

All the slaves had jobs to do. Booker's mother was the cook for the family that owned the plantation. They lived in the big house nearby. She cooked their food over an open fire in her own cabin. So Booker's cabin was warm in winter but too hot in summer.

Sometimes she gave her own family part of a chicken cooked for the big house. More often Booker had a potato or a cup of milk.

Little Booker had many different jobs. He carried water to people in the fields. Each week he took corn to the mill. He had to go through the woods and got home after dark.

The girls in the big house went to school. He had to carry their books. But he could not go inside the school.

In 1865, when Booker was nine, the slaves
were freed. He didn't know what it would mean.
He had heard his mother say prayers in the
night. She had always asked to be free.

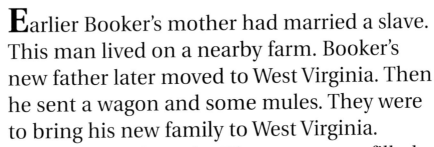

Earlier Booker's mother had married a slave. This man lived on a nearby farm. Booker's new father later moved to West Virginia. Then he sent a wagon and some mules. They were to bring his new family to West Virginia.

The trip took weeks. The wagon was filled with their few things. So the children walked beside it across the mountains. At last they got to Malden, West Virginia. Their house was no better than the one they had left. Maybe it was even worse.

Booker's stepfather worked at a salt mine. He put salt into huge barrels. Booker and his brother, John, got jobs there, too.

One day he saw many people standing
around a young man. The young man was
reading a newspaper to them. They were not
able to read themselves. They listened carefully
to the news. Then Booker knew that learning to
read made people different. It could make a life
different. Booker made up his mind. He would
learn to read! He would learn everything that
he could.

Booker's mother wanted to help. She got him a book called Webster's "Blue-backed Speller." He used it to teach himself the letters. He also knew the number 18. That number was on all the barrels he filled at the salt mines.

Booker wanted to learn much more. A teacher came and started a school nearby. Booker wanted to go. At last his stepfather let him. But Booker had to work five hours before and two hours after school. This was just to make his stepfather let him go.

At school, the teacher asked the children's names. Booker saw that the others had two names. When it was his turn, he answered, "Booker Washington!" Years later he learned his last name was Taliaferro. He kept that as his middle name. He was called Booker T. Washington. And he had learned to read!

Booker Washington wanted more than a full
name. He wanted to keep going to school. But his
stepfather had changed his mind. Now he wanted
Booker to work full time. So Booker left school to
work in the coal mines.

The mines were dark and dirty and not safe.
But when he had time, Booker read his one
book. He used his work lamp for light. At night
he often walked for miles to reach a teacher.

One day some people in the mine talked about Hampton Institute. It was a trade school for blacks. That means it taught what people needed to get good jobs. Booker made up his mind to go to that school.

In 1871 Booker was fifteen. He went to work
for Mrs. Viola Ruffin. She was the wife of the
man who owned the mines. She was hard to
please. But it was better than working in the
coal mines. Booker wanted to give it a try.

Mrs. Ruffin told him to clean out a shed. He
went right to work. Soon he was finished. She
took one look and told him to start over. He did
the job again. She told him it still wasn't good
enough. He did it again. And again. And again.
Then the floor had no spots. The windows were
clean, and the tools were in piles. Mrs. Ruffin
was pleased.

Booker worked for her a year and a half. She couldn't stand to see a single spot. But she talked to him about learning things. And she let him go to school after work.

In the fall of 1872, Booker left for Hampton Institute in eastern Virginia. His mother was sad to see him go. But she wanted him to go to school. He had saved a little money. His neighbors gave him what they could. Still he didn't have enough money to get there. And he didn't have enough to pay for school.

When his money for the stagecoach ran out,
he walked. In the city of Richmond, he had to
sleep under a sidewalk. He had no money for
food. The next morning he found a job loading
a ship. He worked until he had enough money
to get to Hampton.

Many young people wanted to go to Hampton Institute. There was not room enough for everyone. Booker had a meeting with Miss Mackie, the assistant principal. When it was over, she was not sure about him. He would have to work to pay for school. He was dirty and tired. But there was something about Booker. She asked him to wait.

He waited for hours. He had seen some young people get in. Others were turned away. At last Miss Mackie said, "The room next door needs sweeping. Take the broom and sweep it."

Booker remembered what he had learned from books. But he also knew how to do a job well. He swept the room three times. Then he dusted it four times. He moved everything and cleaned under it. He cleaned every corner. Then he told Miss Mackie he was finished.

She rubbed a white handkerchief across a table. She looked everywhere for dirt. Then she smiled. "I guess you will do to enter," she said.

Booker T. Washington did well at Hampton Institute. He learned how to do many jobs. He learned to farm and to make bricks. He learned to give speeches. He also learned arithmetic, science, and history.

After he finished at Hampton, he came back as a teacher. Two years later he was asked to be a principal. He would be at a new school. The school was in Tuskegee, Alabama.

Booker came to Tuskegee in 1881. He found that **HE** was the new school. There were no buildings, no teachers, and no students. But that did not stop him.

He went around the country to find students. He was able to use an old church for the school. When it rained, water poured through the roof. The students held an umbrella over his head. He just went on teaching.

The old church was just the beginning of Tuskegee Institute. Booker T. Washington had great plans for this school.

Tuskegee grew into a school that even Booker could hardly have pictured. By 1915 there were over 100 buildings and about 1,500 students. They could learn 38 jobs and many subjects. They could learn what Booker believed. He felt we get what is worth having in life by hard work.

What students learned at Tuskegee Institute was worth learning. Booker T. Washington always worked hard to teach them.

Key Dates

1856	Born a slave on a plantation in Virginia.
1865	Slaves were freed. He moved with his family to Malden, West Virginia. Booker worked in the mines.
1871	Worked for Mrs. Viola Ruffin, the mine owner's wife. She helped him learn and let him go to school after work.
1872-1875	Attended Hampton Institute in Virginia.
1879	Became a teacher at Hampton Institute.
1881	Became head of Tuskegee Institute in Alabama.
1901	*Up from Slavery*, his famous autobiography, was published.
1915	Died while he was still president of Tuskegee Institute.

Note: Booker T. Washington postage stamp, 1940; his coin—a half dollar, 1946.